INFJ FRIENDSHIPS
Making Real Connections

JENNIFER SOLDNER

INFJ Friendships:

Making Real Connections

First Edition

ISBN 978-1-546-47415-9

Disclaimer:

The information in this book is intended for your general knowledge only and is based solely on the

Dedicated to Wendy D.

"The greatest gift of life is friendship,

and I have received it."

Hubert H. Humphrey

Additional books by

JENNIFER SOLDNER

The Empathic INFJ:

Awareness and Understanding for the Intuitive Clairsentient

The INFJ Heart:

Understand the Mind, Unlock the Heart

A Look Inside a Rare Mind:

An INFJ's Journal through Personal Discovery

CONTENTS

Introduction

Friendship enriches our lives. It allows us to feel connected and accepted, just as we are. It can be like ice on a wound in hardships or sprinkles on a cake in celebration. While it may not make or break our lives, friendship softens our blows and enhances our joys. We see lives around us transformed through friendship and ample evidence toward its importance, but what about those who don't have a lot of friends?

One of the biggest struggles for an INFJ is finding others to connect with at a deeper level; those who will go beyond the shallow chit chat of everyday life and delve deep into soul-inspiring discussions. INFJs often find themselves seeking someone who allows them to show their true selves without feeling the need to hide, conform, or subdue their vibrant inner worlds. They long for a like-minded individual to stumble into their mist, or at the very least, someone that will not judge them for simply being themselves. This type of friend can seem hard, or even impossible, to come by.

Watching others effortlessly show themselves to the world and be accepted baffles the INFJ. It seems so easy for other personality types to click and make friends. They see those easily creating what they pine for and are left wondering what they are doing wrong, or worse, what is wrong with them. Does this sound familiar to you?

In youth, you were considered shy, quiet, or reserved. You may have had one or two people you could tag along with, but you never truly felt understood. Now as an adult, making friends seems even more challenging than before. Where do you find people who will understand you? How do you approach complete strangers and discuss anything more than the weather? How do you expose yourself safely, without the fear of judgment on how you experience the world?

The fact that you have picked up this book is a pretty good sign that you can relate. Perhaps you have some acquaintances but are struggling to find a close friend with whom you can share every intimate detail. Maybe you are seeking insights on how to overcome feelings of loneliness in your everyday life. Or perhaps you have friendships but you are looking for deeper connections. Regardless of your current situation, it is my hope that this book will offer you some insights as to how you can foster deeper connections and release any feelings of loneliness, allowing you to finally make the real connections you seek.

The INFJ Friend

"To be yourself in a world that is constantly trying to make you something else is the greatest accomplishment."
Ralph Waldo Emerson

"Think lightly of yourself and deeply of the world."
Miyamoto Musashi

"It is a most distressing affliction to have a sentimental heart and a skeptical mind."
Naguib Manfouz

The INFJ is thought to be the rarest among the sixteen Myers-Briggs personality types. The acronym stands for Introvert, iNtuitive, Feeling, and Judicial. These four letters make up the cognitive processes which explain how we view and interact with the world around us. According to the Myers & Briggs Foundation, INFJs "seek meaning and connection in ideas, relationships, and material possessions. [They] want to understand what motivates people and are insightful about others."[1] Making up a believed one to three percent[2] of the population, they tend to feel as though they are alone in how they view the world. This perception inhibits their ability to connect with those around them. Often guarded, an INFJ tends to actively distance themselves from those who they believe will not understand them or those with whom they already feel a disconnection.

---

[1] The Myers & Briggs Foundation. "The 16 MBTI Types." 2017. http://www.myersbriggs.org/my-mbti-personality-type/mbti-basics/the-16-mbti-types.htm.
[2] Statistic was "compiled from a variety of MBTI® results from 1972 through 2002, including data banks at the Center for Applications of Psychological Type; CPP, Inc.; and Stanford Research Institute (SRI)." The Myers & Briggs Foundation. "How Frequent is My Type." 2017. http://www.myersbriggs.org/my-mbti-personality-type/my-mbti-results/how-frequent-is-my-type.htm

INFJs crave long term relationships and do not wish to settle for anything less. They only want to pursue friendships which appear to have long term potential, and even then, they tend to be wary for fear that it may all fall apart or they may be betrayed. The INFJ prefers to spend their time with those who share their personal views and values and are slow to expose themselves or their thoughts to others. Their distaste for wasting time on small talk or relationships with no potential to expand combined with their thick, protective outer shell, leave them stuck between a rock and a hard place, unsure of how to establish lasting friendships without wasting mental energy on pointless avenues.

As introverts, they prefer one-on-one encounters as group settings can feel overwhelming and hinder the deep conversations they crave. Not only do they not enjoy the overwhelm of several people talking at once, they also tend to be more reserved and introspective making it difficult for them to speak up among a crowd and interject their points through the rapid paced conversation of a variety of thoughts.

INFJs find themselves to be walking contradictions, loving others but wanting to distance themselves. They have moments of craving interaction but want the freedom to end that interaction when they have had their fill. They want time to themselves but will be ready and on call when a friend is in need. They love to have plans but only when they feel in the mood to have plans. They are quiet and reserved but know how to fly their freak flag. Unlike many other introverted personalities, the INFJ can easily be viewed as an extrovert in the right settings. They have the uncanny ability to leave others thinking that they know all about them when actually, they don't have a clue what is on the inside.

OUTGOING INTROVERTS

Despite the common stereotype associated with the term introvert, the INFJ can crave being with other people. The term introvert is often viewed as one who is antisocial, shy, or dislikes people. This could not be further from the truth. The introvert/extrovert scale as originally defined by Carl Jung,[3] has nothing to do with how outgoing or sociable someone is. Instead, it refers

---

[3] Jung, Carl. *Psychological Types*. Princeton University Press, 1976.

to how we recharge. Extroverts recharge through external stimuli which they gain from interacting with other people. Introverts, on the other hand, recharge from within, gaining their energy from being inside of their own mind.

This reality is hardwired within our bodies. It goes beyond whether or not you enjoy dance clubs or sitting with your cat (by the way, introverts can enjoy both equally). Back in 1999, a study published in the *American Journal of Psychology* tracked and mapped the cerebral blood flow of introverts and extroverts only to discover that their blood actually ran different courses throughout the brain.[4] The key note is that each pathway through which the blood flowed actually required a different neurotransmitter. The pathways used by extroverts require the neurotransmitter dopamine while the pathway used by introverts requires acetylcholine. When we perform activities which get the adrenaline flowing and fill us with positive, rewarding emotions, dopamine is released. This fuels the blood flow of an extrovert, improving their mood, learning,

---

[4] Johnson, D. L., Wiebe, J. S., Gold, S.M., et al. "Cerebral blood flow and personality: a positron emission tomography study." *American Journal of Psychiatry.* Feb. 1999: 156(2):252-7.

memory, and overall cognitive functioning. Extroverts require consistent fills of dopamine in order for their brains to work at an optimum level.

Introverts, on the other hand, need much less dopamine in their systems. Instead, their brains are connected with the energy-conserving neurotransmitter, acetylcholine. While both the introvert and extrovert require acetylcholine and dopamine, the levels of which these neurotransmitters are active within the brain dramatically affects how they feel, think, and behave.

In *The Introvert Advantage*, Marti Olsen Laney discusses this point explaining that the extrovert, who requires a larger amount of dopamine, best gets this through interacting with other people: "Extroverts feel good when they have places to go and people to see."[5]

Even though the extrovert and introvert require different levels of neurotransmitters, there is a necessary balance we all need to maintain in order to function at healthy levels. Too much dopamine, for example, can border on addiction or psychosis while too little, you fall into lethargy or social phobias. The same is true of

---

[5] Olsen Laney, Marti. *The Introvert Advantage: How Quiet People Can Thrive in an Extrovert World.* Workman Publishing Company; 2002.

acetylcholine. Too much can lead to depression while too little can cause dementia and other brain disorders. Human beings are neither best served by being entirely secluded nor continuously exposed. As Jung reportedly stated, "There is no such thing as a pure introvert or extrovert. Such a person would be in the lunatic asylum."

While INFJs may require lower levels of dopamine, they do require it. Any introvert who spends their time in the solitude of their mind deprives themselves of the dopamine release which can best be obtained by getting out and interacting with others. As an INFJ, you have moments when you prefer to hide away, fuel your inner world, and allow for the healthy release of acetylcholine, but when the dopamine begins to wane, you feel the call to get out and socialize. During these times, you may find yourself behaving more like the life of the party, excited to socialize and bond in friendship.

On top of this biochemical hardwiring, INFJs go a step further in their longing to connect with others. The MBTI personality type is a roadmap to understanding the functions of the brain. As an NF temperament, as defined by Dr. David Keirsey, "tend to be giving, trusting, spiritual, and they are focused on personal journeys and human potentials."[6] This aspect of the INFJ leads them to want to help others. Feeling deep connections goes beyond their need for dopamine and reaches deeper into their desire to uplift those around them for the good of everyone involved. Dr. A.J. Drenth, author of *My True Type*, once stated that "INFJs often feel happiest and most fulfilled when helping others understand themselves and their problems."[7]

This piece of the INFJ personality is what fuels their love of interacting, causing them to appear as extroverts to the outside world. But this same outward focus is what keeps them feeling lonely and misunderstood. While they enjoy every moment of helping another, connecting with them on the depth of their problems, and offering advice, empathy, and insight when they can, this behavior is usually not reciprocated. The INFJ still shields their inner world and hides their

---

[6] Synergy Leaders, LLC. (A division of Kiersey.com). "The Idealists." 2017. http://www.keirsey.com/synergyleaders/overview_idealist.aspx

[7] Drenth, A.J. *My True Type: Clarifying Your Personality Type, Preferences & Functions.* Inquire Books; 2014.

own struggles, leaving them with feelings of loneliness even after a dopamine-enriching night out.

Ultimately, going out and seeking fulfillment of their craving for social interaction leaves them feeling emptier than before they left the house. The dopamine overload drains them and they did not make the connections for which they had hoped. Now, back at home, they wonder if they will ever find that real, meaningful connection. This endless cycle of socializing continues each time that craving to be with others pops up, but no true friendship emerges. Conversations are either superficial and empty or they are deep and one-sided, neither of which allow the INFJ any hope for a healthy, mutual future friendship.

While INFJs have very specific needs and wants within a friendship, this does not have to leave them hopeless in their search for finding meaningful connections. With the appropriate mindset and armed with some knowledge and tools, INFJs are more than capable of fulfilling their need for connection while remaining true to who they are.

The Marathon

*"Be slow to fall into friendship; but when thou art in,
continue firm and constant."*
Socrates

*"Most people are enduring a marginalized isolation. One
of the great obstacles to modern friendships is the
'religion of rush.' People are rushing all the time through
time. Friendship takes time."*
John O'Donohue

*"Even where friendship is concerned, it takes me a long
time to trust people."*
Namie Amuro

Friendship is a staple of life. Each and every human being craves another soul with which to connect. The absence of friendship is painful, and when something hurts, we want instant relief.

When you visualize the perfect friend, and think about the relationship you desire filled with give and take, deep understanding, camaraderie, and having one another's backs, you can feel in your heart that you want that tomorrow. The longing of friendship usually does not call to mind uncomfortable conversations or discussions of the weather. It doesn't bring up hours of wondering if the person before you is trustworthy, if they are on the same page as you, or if they hold beliefs which passionately contradict your own.

You want comfort and you want warmth. You want to end the pain of feeling lonely and fill a very specific void. So when you say that you want to make a friend, you are really saying you want to go from zero to hero yesterday.

It is completely understandable to feel this way, and a normal response to a longing desire. When one wants to lose one hundred pounds, they are visualizing the joy of being one hundred pounds lighter rather than the pain of slowly losing a pound here or there and occasionally gaining one back. A person with big dreams to pay off all of their debts fantasizes about the ample money in their bank account. They are not as keen on looking at clipping coupons or abstaining from buying the latest luxuries.

Desire is an amazing thing because it tells us exactly what we want. It keeps us focused on the goal in order to endure the moments that seem less than thrilling. It reminds us that we are working toward easing the pain as we endure the minor discomforts. Much like a sore deep tissue massage will yield glorious days of lessened back pain, the discomfort of hours of small talk opens up the opportunity for relieving long term loneliness.

Friendship is a marathon and not a sprint. There is no true lasting friendship that occurs overnight and it is necessary to take things slow in order to cultivate what you crave. In the moment of loneliness, it is easy to slip into going full force into friendships with the wrong people. You may find yourself clinging to those individuals who ignite a fire within you in the moment and make you feel alive and excited, ignoring the red flags or characteristics which oppose your desires only to find later, when you need them, they are nowhere to be seen.

Perhaps in your longing to fill the void of friendship, you find yourself behaving like someone you are not. You seek to people-please and "fit in," feeling as though this is the only way to create friendships, leaving you surrounded by people but lonelier than when you began. These things are merely band aids over a serious wound. They will never fix the problem and are more likely to push the truth of the pain out of view, worsening the underlying problem over time. There is no quick fix when it comes to lasting, fulfilling friendships.

The goal to the type of connection you desire means time and patience. It means enduring discomfort, allowing those to come and go, and continuing to push through in faith that what you seek is, in fact, out there. There is no quick fix when it comes to obtaining friendships. As we continue forward in this book, we will take a look at ways that you can ease the pain of loneliness to allow yourself the ability to slow down and cultivate healthy friendships.

A Healthy Dance

"When we honestly ask ourselves which person in our lives means the most to us, we often find that it is those who, instead of giving advice, solutions, or cures, have chosen rather to share our pain and touch our wounds with a warm and tender hand."
Henri Nouwen

"Friendship will not stand the strain of very much good advice for very long."
Robert Staughton Lynd

"A friend is someone who gives you total freedom to be yourself."
Jim Morrison

Before we can move forward discussing how to build real connections and foster deep friendships, it is necessary to look at what a healthy friendship is and how we can avoid falling into codependent or unhealthy patterns. As I already mentioned, looking for a friendship to fill emotional voids can land us in relationships that are less than fulfilling, leaving us drained and still alone. For this reason, the first step to seeking friendships is to understand that no friendship can fill a void within us. It is our responsibility to fill ourselves before looking to connect with others. Only in this manner can we find others who are fulfilled and not looking for us to complete them. Every individual is complete on their own. Through this completeness, we can enjoy one another's company without putting unhealthy expectations on them or allowing them to put their emotional responsibilities onto us.

INFJs are helpers. We love helping others and have a unique ability to notice where someone is struggling and see the bigger picture, offering them advice and guidance to work through their problems. INFJs often feel most fulfilled when they are able to help another. In friendships, this can be one of our greatest assets when used appropriately. However, the very quality that makes us wonderful friends can easily turn into the thing that pushes others away. The key point to remember is that, despite how great you are at helping others, it is not your job to fix them. Whether you want to or whether they ask you to, it is never your responsibility to solve their problems.

Friendships are wonderful for relying on one another and assisting through the hardships, and a healthy friendship can flourish with the give and take of welcomed advice, but use caution when advice giving or problem solving becomes the crutch of the friendship.

SIGNS OF CODEPENDENCE

Codependence occurs within a relationship when responsibility for problems and emotional health is no longer falling in the right places. It happens when one person feels or is made to be emotionally responsible for another. Each person in a friendship is accountable for how they feel and how they behave at any given time, regardless of the actions or feelings of another.

INFJs can fall into codependent friendships when they begin to feel responsible for fixing someone else or if they do not feel fulfilled unless they are trying to solve another's problems. These types of friendships almost always lead to feelings of bitterness or being taken advantage of. To prevent this from occurring, it is helpful to recognize some of the earlier signs that a friendship is taking a codependent turn.

You feel worse when trying to help. When you are helping another, even though you may feel a little pride in your ability to assist them, you ultimately end up feeling worse. Drained, empty, or depressed, you are left feeling like you either didn't do enough or you were unsuccessful in your attempts to assist. You begin to feel resentful that every conversation is about their problems and you start to feel worse in their presence. You feel guilty if you are not available when they need you, but feel lighter when they are not around.

You feel responsible for the outcome. When you feel responsible for the outcome of aiding another, you feel powerless and at the whim of their choices. You wind up helping from a place that believes they are incapable of helping themselves, disempowering them and perceiving them to be dependent upon you. Your goal becomes focused on improving how they feel so that you can feel better, too. This dance creates an unhealthy and perpetual cycle that only exacerbates negative emotions within the friendship.

They think only you can help them or you think only you can help them. They come to you pleading for your assistance, dismissing you and your feelings, and expect you to help them. They may even leave you feeling guilty if you are unable to offer them your time or energy, making you feel solely responsible for their continued suffering. You find yourself feeling as though you must be available to help whenever they need you out of fear that any negative outcome is your fault. You worry that you need to do more lest their problems grow worse. Rather than being there as a friend because you want to be, you are there because you feel obligated.

The majority of time is focused on their problems. Friendships are built on mutual exchanges.

If you find that the majority of your get togethers are spent focusing on their problems or complaints, then the friendship may not be very balanced. If they continually come to you to complain but never take your advice or take any steps in a direction to improve their situation, the friendship has shifted from comfort and camaraderie to therapy sessions.

You only feel good when you have succeeded in helping them. It is natural to feel good when you see another's success, but if you only feel good when you are trying to improve another's life, then you are making how you feel conditional upon the actions of another. You become too dependent on the outcome of your advice and are more likely to meddle where you shouldn't be. No one's success can be dependent upon anyone else, and if you operate from this place, then you will find yourself in enabling and codependent friendships.

If you look back at your friendships and find the majority of these points to be fitting, then it is possible you have been nurturing imbalanced friendships where each person is relying too heavily upon the other. These may feel good in the short term but almost always lead to burn out and feelings of loneliness.

If you have patterns of these types of friendships, you may benefit from seeking professional assistance to delve further into the root of these patterns and understand how you can change them. Codependency may have many different causes stemming from your youth and adult life that a trained therapist can aid you in working through. Often times, codependent behavior can be the result of believing you need another to feel fulfilled. In these instances, reaching a place where you can soothe your own feelings of loneliness will allow you to slow down and approach friendships from a healthier place.

Unconditional Connection

"The best time to make friends is before you need them."
Ethel Barrymore

"Even though everybody's lives are different, in general we're all human beings, and we go through the same things: disappointments, the pleasures of life, life and death."
Joan Jett

"I believe in the goodness of man, and I believe we're all connected... We have our differences. But if we will recognize that we like each other, that we are more common than uncommon, we will work toward what needs to be done to reconcile that."
Corbin Bernsen

I know you may be thinking that it is too hard to wait for the perfect friendship. After all, you are lonely now. You want someone now to help you when you are down and share in your joys. How can you wait for the pure friendship you desire when you are in discomfort where you currently stand? How can you get to a place where you can stop the bleeding of the wound without hiding it behind a band aid?

The first step is understanding that friendship may not hold the key to unlocking all of your happiness. Even if you were to find the perfect friend tomorrow, you would still find yourself dealing with the very same emotions with which you are currently struggling, including loneliness, feelings of separation, and sadness. Friendship brings with it glorious transformations and benefits, but we cannot reap these benefits unless we are able to stand in a good place without them.

Loneliness is not caused by a lack of people in our lives. We can be surrounded by people, good people, of whom we love and connect with, and still feel loneliness deep within ourselves. The reality is that loneliness is not based in quantity or even quality of people around us but rather in perception. How we perceive our current circumstances is what creates feelings of loneliness within us.

When we perceive ourselves as lonely, we feel disconnected from those around us. We begin to think that no one will understand us and therefore we can never fit in. Terms like misfit or the black sheep are fitting to our emotional situation and we render ourselves hopeless of any real connection. Finding others that fit perfectly with our views and beliefs, those with whom we long to connect, will only worsen our feelings of loneliness as we perceive ourselves as incapable of connecting to others.

By feeling lonely and perceiving your current state as lonesome, you inhibit your ability to notice or think of opportunities in which you can lessen these emotions and therefore making it impossible to find new friends.

In believing that finding friends will cure our perception of loneliness, we create an endless cycle. As we feel lonely, we miss opportunities. As opportunities are missed, we feel hopeless in finding friends. When we cannot find friends, we feel lonelier and thus the cycle goes on.

The only way to jump off of this rollercoaster is to cure the feelings of loneliness without the condition of another. That is, to find a way to feel fulfilled and connected to those around us without seeking a specific person to appear in our lives or behave in such a way that we are able to feel connected.

On the one hand, this realization is empowering. It reminds us that we are in complete control of our emotional state regardless of who is in our lives and how they may think or behave. However, it can be frightening as we now seek to choose feelings of connectedness without being sure with whom to connect.

Once you have recognized that loneliness is a state of perception and has nothing to do with how many or how few people are surrounding you, you can then begin to take that out of the equation of friendship. By working to removing the feelings of loneliness, you are better able to soothe the discomfort which causes you to rush into less fulfilling friendships. This slows the desperate feelings of your timeframe and makes you better able to objectively look at those around you, allowing for more conversation, slower engagements, and longer lasting foundations of friendship.

Think about soothing the pain of loneliness as applying a numbing agent to the wound. You haven't used a band aid to cover it up, nor have you solved the problem entirely, but you have now created a space for yourself to work on healing the wound in an effective and appropriate manner, not stemming from rush or desperation.

This soothing, of course, is easier said than done, especially when we have spent a lifetime cultivating the habit of loneliness. The key is focusing on the thoughts which you are thinking and shifting them to productive and beneficial thoughts. Use your emotions as a guideline to determine whether your thoughts are benefiting you or hurting you; making you feel more connected or less connected. It is not necessary to have any one specific individual in mind to think thoughts which allow you to feel more connected to those around you. You can be general in your thinking and still shift yourself to recognizing how connected you really are in your day to day life. You can do this as a daily exercise in order to cultivate a new habit of thought.

CONNECTEDNESS EXERCISE

Consider setting aside some time, thirty minutes will do, where you can actively focus on your thoughts and work through which ones make you feel more connected and which lend themselves to feelings of loneliness. By doing this exercise regularly, you will begin to see that you do not, in fact, need someone else in your life in order to decrease your feelings of loneliness. Of course, this is not meant to replace seeking out new friendships, as friendship and community are healthy and beneficial, but rather to show you that you are capable of feeling better by yourself, thus decreasing feelings of neediness and codependence, making you attract healthier individuals and be more open to slow relationship building.

In this thirty minute exercise, it may help to have a pen and paper handy in order to make notes of which thoughts feel better and more connected and which thoughts increase loneliness. This will make it simpler next time as you can jump right to the thoughts that you know work well. Before you begin, consider where you are right now in your emotions. Maybe jot down a place on a scale of one to ten; one representing extreme loneliness and ten representing feeling deeply connected. If you wish to take it further, try writing down a sentence that sums up what you believe in this moment. For example, if you peg yourself at one on the scale, your sentence may be something like, "I have absolutely no one in my life that understands me or even wants to be around me." If you select ten, your sentence would probably be closer to, "I have many people who I can connect with in my life and they enjoy my presence." It is also possible to be higher on the scale and have a sentence that does not refer to specific friendships such as, "There are so many people in the world that are just like me in that they [insert reason] and I know the perfect friendship is on its way." If you are feeling somewhere in between, write down a sentence that applies. The idea is that your sentence sums up your current beliefs about your situation. Be as honest as possible with yourself. Noting your true beliefs is the only way to shift those beliefs and therefore shift how you feel about your present moment.

Once you have your number on the scale and a sentence that sums up what you believe about this moment, it is time to slowly start pushing yourself up the scale. If you are already at a ten, great! This exercise will only enhance those emotions by confirming your current beliefs. If you are at a lower number, then the goal will be to work your way up the scale until you feel more connected. Do not worry about moving up to a ten if you are only at a five. Any progress up the scale is worth celebrating.

Now you are ready to play with your thoughts. There are no wrong thoughts here. The key is to think things you actually believe. If you think outlandish thoughts which you do not believe, then this exercise will not change your feelings. Avoid thoughts like, "I will meet my best friend tomorrow!" as you obviously would struggle to believe this. Play with your thoughts and notice how each one makes you feel. Try beginning with two strong opposing thoughts to feel the difference. "No one gets me" is one you may currently believe. Notice how you feel as you focus on this thought. Does it make you feel disconnected, hopeless, and otherwise negative? Now think of an opposing thought which is believable to you: "There are other people out there who feel lonely sometimes, too." Notice how this thought feels. Does it feel better or worse? Do you feel slight relief in thinking it? Does it help you feel more connected and less alone?

Continue on in this way, paying close attention to your emotions and thinking on a thought long enough to figure out if it makes you feel better or worse. The more you begin to hone in on the types of thoughts that feel better, the easier it will become to think more thoughts of that nature. Once you are on a roll, you may find yourself on an uplifting run of talking yourself into positive, soothing thoughts.

The more you can practice thinking thoughts that make you feel better and bring you relief and a sense of connection to the world around you, the more likely these are to become your default thoughts. Even though you have yet to find someone who understands you or allows you to be completely yourself, you can turn to your own mind and feel a sense of acceptance and understanding.

Like Attracts Like

"Like attracts like. Just be who you are, calm and clear and bright. Automatically, as we shine who we are, asking ourselves every minute is this what I really want to do, doing it only when we answer yes, automatically that turns away those who have nothing to learn from who we are, and attracts those who do, and from whom we have to learn, as well."
Richard Bach

"The first step to getting what you want is to have the courage to get rid of what you don't."
Zig Ziglar

"My life is good because I am not passive about it. I invest in what is real. Like real people, to do real things, for the real me."
Gwyneth Paltrow

As you work on your feelings of loneliness and desperation, you will find yourself attracting those who are less needy and therefore more emotionally capable of a fulfilling relationship. The simple truth is that we attract what we are, not what we want. So when you are feeling desperate for friendship and clinging to those who quickly fill the void, you wind up attracting others who are seeking outside people to ease their own pains.

INFJs, being ones who not only love helping others but are very good at offering aid to those who are suffering, can end up in unhealthy friendships as they attract those wishing to be fulfilled by another. While they are longing to ease their despair, the INFJ is quick to assist them. This balance works for a short period of time as both parties feel fulfilled, needed, and wanted. But over time, the INFJ starts to feel drained, used, and maybe even bitter. When they seek to have their needs met, looking for assistance with a problem, sharing their emotions, or simply hoping for a shoulder to lean on, the original balance of the friendship is thrown off kilter and the INFJ finds themselves feeling alone while the needy friend feels angry that their needs are no longer front and center. This relationship creates an unhealthy codependent cycle, one that is difficult for the INFJ to break free from, particularly if feelings of loneliness persist.

Rather, as we work on our own perception and freeing ourselves from needing the friendship of another to fulfill us, we will begin to attract those who feel the same way. In this manner, both are fulfilled through their own thinking and feeling and can then come together in a beautiful harmony of support and understanding. This is the basis of healthy friendships.

As we attract what we are, we must look at what prevents us from finding true friendships and notice that others are out there doing the same. In order to make new relationships in our lives, we must obviously encounter new people. This requires us to go out to social locations, make attempts to interact with others, and follow up with those with which we feel comfortable.

Each of these steps proves painful for the INFJ. Heading out to social events can often be a struggle for a variety of reasons. The introvert in us becomes rapidly drained from a large gathering. We may find ourselves anxious or uncomfortable in new situations, or even overwhelmed and overstimulated from loud noises and excessive energies. As our personality type is hyper sensitive to the emotions of those around us, large crowds have us so focused on others that making the effort to pay attention to our own actions can prove too much, therefore approaching strangers, coming up with things to say, and carrying on any sort of small talk are the last thing we want to do. Even if we do manage to connect with someone at a social gathering, it is not uncommon for INFJs to passively leave the encounter as it was, hoping for the other person to reach out, fearing that if we reach out to them, we may be bothering them or interrupting their presumably already fulfilling life.

So instead, the scenario plays out in one of three ways:

- The INFJ manages to attend a social gathering and the only person they wind up interacting with is an outgoing type who approaches them, eager to talk to someone. This person winds up filling most of the conversational air, offering further avenues for contact, following up the next day, and the day after, and the day after. This causes the INFJ to feel smothered but hesitant to place any distance on the friendship. Overall, it becomes an imbalanced transfer of emotional energy.

- The INFJ manages to make a brilliant connection with someone at the gathering. They spend hours talking and connecting, with a conversation filled with "me toos!" After phone numbers and emails are exchanged, they then both anxiously await the other to contact them, neither doing so, both thinking the other person didn't have that great of a time after all.

- The INFJ makes their way to the social gathering and sits with a beverage watching as those around them interact. They make occasional pleasantries, and then head home feeling as though no one else wishes to connect on the deep level for which they long. All the while unaware of the fact that another likeminded individual was sitting at the gathering doing the exact same thing.

You will note in these scenarios the passivity of the INFJ. You may be able to relate. You want to make friends and connect with those who are just like you, but those who are just like you are also sitting passively with similar thoughts, hoping for someone just like them to make the first move.

We attract what we are and if what we are is someone who is fearful, hesitant, or concerned with making the first move, then those we attract around us will be doing the same. At the local coffee shop, in the bookstores, sitting beside us in the classroom, and all around us at every moment are many others, just like you, who are longing to make real connections and be understood, but are too afraid to make the first move or allow themselves to be vulnerable.

Get Clear

"Wishing to be friends is quick work, but friendship is a slow ripening fruit."
Aristotle

"At the center of your being you have the answer; you know who you are and you know what you want."
Lao Tzu

"If you don't know what you want, you end up with a lot you don't."
Chuck Palahniuk

"If you really know... what you want and how to get there, then everything else really falls into place."
Marlen Esparza

The reality of life is that you cannot achieve what you do not know you want. "But I know what I want," you may say. "I want a good friend." This is very well true, but it is as vague as you can possibly get. If you wanted to buy a house, would you simply say, "I want a house," and hope that the rest filled itself in? Odds are you would not wind up with a house you enjoyed when it was all said and done. Instead, if you look through magazines, browse open houses, or search images online, you would begin to notice what you really want in a home. You would start to think of what needs you want the house to fill and then adjust your searches accordingly. Ultimately, you would have a pretty specific idea in mind of the house you wished to purchase. This clear knowing of what you want would guide you toward houses you preferred and away from those that didn't meet your needs. Friendship is the same way.

You know that you want a close, healthy friendship, but if you aren't clear on exactly what you want in this friendship, then you may wind up with one that is far from what you had hoped. Just as you would dream of an ideal home, take some time to dream of an ideal friendship. Ask yourself what you want in a best friend. Try to visualize an avatar of precisely who you wish to spend your time with. Don't worry about being realistic in this exercise. Go ahead and be as picky as you want to be.

Vague and altruistic qualities are great to include if they are important to you, but don't limit yourself to "nice" or "empathetic." Get more specific and think of superficial qualities that you enjoy simply for the sake of enjoying them. Do you want them to be fun, exciting, extroverted, or the life of the party? Or perhaps you prefer someone who is consistently low key, quiet, and introspective. Maybe you want someone who is capable of achieving both ends of these extremes. Are you looking for someone who is very similar to you or someone completely opposite? Do you want a friend who instantly gets you or a friend that is open to you explaining who you are? What types of hobbies do you want to connect with this person on? Do you wish to have a lot in common or would you rather they like different activities so you can share new ideas with one another?

Once you have a clear avatar of the perfect friend to call to mind, move onto visualizing the perfect day with this person. Again, we are not reaching for realistic. Clear out any limiting beliefs or boundaries that would prevent you from achieving this perfect day. This is all in your mind, so let yourself create the fantasy you want. Think of it as planning a platonic date. Do you just want to hang out and chat? If so, where? At the beach or coffee shop? Maybe just sitting on your couch? What topics would your conversations include? Maybe you would rather go biking or to a movie or even an art gallery. Think of something you have been dying to share with another and visualize yourself sharing it.

Through this visualization exercise, you have now captured the emotion you are striving for from a friendship. This emotion is key. Hold it in your mind as you think of past attempts at forming friendships. Did any of them bring you to this feeling or did you find them draining, dull, or otherwise lacking? By getting clear on how you want to feel when you are in an ideal friendship, you have established a destination. You have given yourself a clear goal rather than floundering around and hoping another will show you the way to a healthy friendship. You can now use your emotions and your own established set point to navigate your way to a fulfilling friendship.

Reach for this visualization and feeling often. The more you do it, the more you will establish a connection with it. This will make you more sensitive to how you feel when you are getting closer to this reality or when you begin to veer from it.

Think of this emotion as a giant red X on a map, marking the spot of where you want to be. Every road on this map will either bring you toward this X or away from it. When you connect with someone that makes you feel glimpses of this same emotion, you will know that you have found a road on the way toward your red X. Those who make you feel emotions other than what you have specified in your ideal friendship are probably roads that are leading you away from your X. Consider slapping a proverbial "Do Not Enter" sign on those roads in order to keep you on track.

Remember as you feel emotions on the right track, this does not mean that you have arrived at your desired location. If you are in Los Angeles, California and you want to head to Austin, Texas, seeing a sign that says you are headed east is not that same as a sign that says "Welcome to Austin." You want to enjoy the signs that you are on your way in the right direction and continue moving that way. But pretending you have entered Austin when you have simply crossed the border into Nevada is far from healthy and will not yield that true experience you desire.

The same is true for your friendships. Feeling an emotion similar to that which you visualized with your best friend avatar does not mean that you are instantly best friends with this person. To jump to that place is unhealthy and won't yield the friendship results you are seeking. Rather, get excited that you are on your way just like a sign that says east. Continue to visualize where you want to be and continue to pay attention to how you feel with that person. Even though you are heading east, there are still several ways to not reach Austin. That is not meant to discourage when you feel good emotions because there are several ways to get to Austin, too. You don't need to take the fastest route in order to ultimately get there. Rather, it is meant to remind to you to enjoy the signs that you're on your way to building a great friendship while continuing to check that you are headed in the right direction of what you want.

SEEING THE POSSIBILITIES

Now that you have the idea of the friendship you want and how it will feel to have it, you need to believe it is possible to achieve it. You need to recognize that your ideal friendship is in fact on the same continent and not on a different planet.

You may be thinking that you already know how you will feel with an ideal friendship but that friendship just does not exist. You will point to your past as proof that you have been trying to reach Austin for years but you just end up circling Los Angeles. When all of our experience points to one outcome, believing that it could ever be different takes nothing less than a complete mental overhaul.

But remember, you are not the same person you were yesterday. Every single day you are changing and growing, becoming a new person, and so is everyone around you. Every single day in the most unexpected ways there are new opportunities to create lifelong friendships. The past cannot predict that future. If you were able to predict when you would find the perfect friend, you would not be reading this book. But you cannot predict when the friendship you seek will fall into your lap, so why live your life as if you are predicting that it never will?

At this moment, odds are that you do not have the friendship that you want in your life and so visualizing that friendship may feel uncomfortable as it causes you to be painfully aware of its absence within your life. This places you in a state of emotional desperation that causes you to head west on your friendship map rather than east simply because the act of going anywhere feels better than being stuck in one place. But before you know it, this desperation has you flailing around in the depth of the ocean, feeling more frustrated and exhausted than had you just stayed put.

By focusing on thoughts that help you believe the friendship of your dreams is possible, you can shift out of those feelings of desperation that cause you to do anything to fix its absence and into feelings of hope. When we feel hopeful about something, visualizing it and focusing on what it will be like proves more beneficial. We are able to feel more content with where we are and patiently await where we can one day be, ceasing desperate action for the sake of action.

Think about how it feels to want a vacation but have no idea when or how to make it happen. Believing it is impossible makes your current state less bearable or even agonizing. But now think of how it feels when you have already planned, booked, and paid for that vacation. You know for a fact that you will be enjoying that getaway in just a couple of months. Now your current reality doesn't feel as bad when you visualize a vacation because you can reach for that hope and excitement of your sure-thing vacation any time you want.

This is the difference between belief and desire. Desiring a friendship and never knowing when it is coming is painful and places all of your focus and action in desperation of attaining something you don't believe is attainable. Belief that the perfect friendship is coming feels better and puts you in a state of patiently allowing the friendship to unfold while remaining aware of the opportunities around you.

So how do you believe? Begin by recognizing that a belief is simply a thought that you keep thinking.

Past experiences based on your past beliefs caused outcomes that only perpetuated those thoughts and further established those beliefs. But again, you are a completely different person today than you were even a few weeks ago so those beliefs, experiences, and thoughts are no longer serving you. Those habits of thought that were established overtime and have spent a great deal thinking on are possible to change. Thoughts like, "I am so different from those around me" or "no one will ever understand me" are only perpetuating past beliefs and are getting you nowhere. Changing these beliefs will not happen overnight, just as establishing them did not happen overnight. To begin shifting these views, you need to think of the world in a different way. You have seen all the proof in favor of your beliefs, but what if there was proof that your beliefs are inaccurate?

Before we do this, I want to make a note to remember that the point to changing your beliefs on friendships is not meant to be a magical cure but instead to help you calm your current emotional state in order to relax into where you are and offer hope of where you want to be to cease unhelpful, desperate action and open you up to opportunities and possibilities you may otherwise miss. If you are trying to catch a bus to Austin but are unsure of when it will arrive at which station, you wind up running from one bus station to the next, causing you to miss the bus heading the way you want. If, instead, you pick a comfortable location in one station, grab a cup of coffee and relax, you will find that the you are able to take the necessary, productive actions to find the right bus.

With that said, let's take a look at your beliefs. Similar to our earlier exercise of writing down your current thoughts, you need to identify what you believe that is holding you in a place of thinking you can never connect with others. As you look back on that exercise or write down a new list of current beliefs, consider what the underlying theme is in your belief system. Odds are the beliefs stem from one core thought: no one understands me (i.e. I'm too different). Let us take a moment to look at this belief in a different light. In other words, let's try to prove it wrong.

THE COMMON INFJ

The INFJ personality type is known for being the rarest type. The statistics may be difficult to pinpoint, but the general consensus places INFJs as making up only one to three percent of the world's population. If you are an INFJ male, you can cut those numbers in half. When you look at that as a slice of one hundred percent, that is a pretty bleak number when you are hoping to find people who get you. It is no wonder you have formed the belief that no one understands you.

But let us look at these numbers from a different perspective. There are currently 7.5 billion people on the planet. Taking the low end statistic of only one percent of that number means that there are 75 million INFJs in the world. That is a lot of people who understand what it is like to think like you do. It suddenly doesn't sound so bleak, does it?

Allow me to give you another more visual perspective. Let's look at redheads. I am sure you see redheads often at the supermarket, restaurants, or maybe even at your place of work. If someone told you that you would see a couple of redheads within the next week, odds are that you would agree with them. If you made it a point to notice redheads, you would probably be astonished by how many you bump into on a regular basis.

Now what if I told you that redheads make up only one to three percent of the population? It is the truth. The exact same percentage as INFJs and yet you see them all the time. Granted, you do see more blondes and brunettes, but if your goal was to find a redhead, it wouldn't take you long to spot one.

The same is true for INFJs. They might not be as common as other personality types, but odds are that you encounter a couple every week without even noticing it. Just as you don't broadcast your personality type, they aren't flashing a beacon either. But the reality is that you encounter several people throughout the week that understand what it means to live as an INFJ in the world. When you find yourself re-thinking those same unhelpful thoughts that no one understands you or that you are too different to meet anyone like you, just think of the number 75 million and take a look around you. People just like you are everywhere.

Connecting with the World

"There are no strangers here; only friends you haven't yet met."
William Butler Yeats

"Vulnerability is the birthplace of connection and the path to the feeling of worthiness. If it doesn't feel vulnerable, the sharing is probably not constructive."
Brene Brown

"There are days when solitude is a heady wine that intoxicates you with freedom, others when it is a bitter tonic, and still others when it is a poison that makes you beat your head against the wall."
Sidonie Gabrielle Colette

Now that you have come to see that you are not as different from those around you as you once thought, you are probably asking how you can spot these INFJs as easily as you spot a redhead. Life would be a whole lot easier if they just held up a sign or flashed a hand signal so you could get right to the heart of a good conversation. Could you imagine skipping over talks of the weather or local news and jumping right into a discussion on Myers-Briggs personality types? It sounds like a dream but it can be a reality. Instead of wishing other INFJs were easy to spot, take action and make yourself a shining beacon for others like you using a technique I like to call "the soft opener."

THE SOFT OPENER

If you are looking to meet someone who thinks like you, you are going to have to be the one flashing that beacon. Waiting and hoping for others to spontaneously open up to you when you are not willing to do the same will leave you both sitting in stalemate, longing for connection. Now it may not feel comfortable approaching someone else and saying, "Hey, I'm an INFJ. Are you?" That is a sure fire way to glean some uncomfortable looks and cause you to retreat back into your introvert hole, never to try again.

Instead, consider using the soft opener. The soft opener is when you sport something that opens up conversation with likeminded people without any effort from you. You may be using this technique already without even noticing it. Wearing a t-shirt of your favorite sports team, carrying a book title side out, or even putting a passionate or humorous bumper sticker on your car are all soft openers. They are showing the world something about you, allowing them to feel instantly comfortable discussing it if they are on the same page.

You can do this for many different areas of your life; whether book interests, politics, spiritual beliefs, or even hitting right to the heart of it with your personality type. There are plenty of t-shirts out there for Myers-Briggs personalities and introverts. Pick one that speaks the most to you and when you feel in a sociable, outgoing mood, toss it on and head to the park, store, or local coffee shop. Make sure the shirt is clear and easy to read. It may take a time or two out before someone notices or approaches you. They may not be an INFJ, but if they understand your shirt, they are ready to discuss personalities and from there, you have an instant conversation topic with a complete stranger.

The soft opener is perfect for any time you are looking to connect on a specific subject. Take the pressure off of yourself and off of others by advertising exactly what you are looking for. Maybe you love a certain book genre or have a hobby you're passionately into. It does not matter what on subject you are looking to connect with others; the soft opener makes it easy for everyone involved. If you can't find a shirt or bumper sticker that speaks to the subject you want, make your own. There is no shortage of print-on-demand sites that can get you a shirt, sticker, mug, or notebook for under $20. No need for design experience, just pick a word and write it on a shirt of your color choice. Make it clear and obvious to other likeminded people and you've created a soft opener.

The best part is that the soft opener is always within your control. If you don't feel like socializing, don't wear it that day. Bring along a sweatshirt to cover it when you have had enough conversation. You will never need to approach another again as you watch the conversations open up effortlessly before you.

GO FURTHER WITH BABY STEPS

The soft opener is a great way to take the pressure off of you, but it still offers others control over the conversation. There are those who may see a shirt, snicker to themselves, and still not feel comfortable approaching you and you may see others with whom you wish to connect but they don't seem to be interested in your soft opener. In these cases, it is necessary to practice approaching complete strangers. After all, a stranger is simply a friend you haven't met yet, right? As cheesy as it sounds, it is true. If you take a look at your current circle of people and don't see that friendship you seek within it, then the truth is that you need to connect with complete strangers. The more people you connect with, the more likely you are to find people you enjoy. It is just simple math.

In order to find these people, you need to feel comfortable approaching as many complete strangers as possible in a variety of situations. There is a belief that when it comes to socializing, you either have it or you don't. You can think back to your school age experiences and recall those who just seemed to have a charisma about them, charming the lunch lady and chatting with other students from all walks of life. You probably thought that they were born that way, but the truth is that anyone can learn those same techniques.

Do not think of it as attempting to change your personality. This is not the goal at all. You still want to be you, you just want other people to see that real you. Approaching complete strangers is something most of us are not accustomed to. Very few people, especially introverts, tend to go around attempting to talk with as many strangers as possible. But the fastest way to find friendship is through this very technique. It takes practice, but the more you practice it, the easier it will become and before you know it, approaching those you have never met will feel like second nature. To begin practicing, use baby steps. These baby steps are broken up in a way that you can practice one until you feel completely comfortable before moving onto the next. Each step piggy backs on the one before it and none are designed to shock your social system or cripple you in anxiety.

Before we get to these steps, it is important to address the reality of an INFJ's social quota. INFJs are introverts, but despite the stereotype that introverts either don't like people or prefer to not be around them, the INFJ craves human contact. This craving can be beneficial when you have had plenty of introverted time to recharge and have a close friend or group that you can jump right into when you feel the craving hit. But this ideal situation is rare when you throw in work life, school life, family life, and all else life throws at us. You wind up with three factors constantly fluctuating on a sliding scale:

Drained ←→ Recharged

Socially satisfied ←→ Craving interaction

Lonely ←→ Connected

These factors emerge in a variety of ways. You wind up in stages that look something like this:

- Craving social interaction but too emotionally exhausted to get off the couch.

- Stuck in a social situation but longing to get away to recharge.

- Feeling charged up but have no one to connect with and nowhere to go.

- Socially filled and at peace while you relax on your couch in solitude.

- Excited to go out and have fun with your favorite friends.

There are many variations of the sliding scales, but these are some of the most common. Some may relate to one scenario more than the others and there might be scenarios that you have never or rarely experienced given your individual circumstances. Every human has these three sliding scales but we are going to focus on how they affect the INFJ specifically.

As introverts with a craving for social interaction and the ability to only feel a deep connection with a select few, the INFJ spends a great deal of time in uncomfortable places on these sliding scales. It seems that none of the scales line up in a manner to create the perfect sense of social pleasure. Perhaps we make plans when we are feeling and craving social interaction only for that day to arrive and now we are drained and dreading it. This causes us to back out of the plans, but our craving never gets fulfilled. By the time we have had a chance to recharge, everyone else is busy and we are stuck with no one to see.

The most comfortable position when it comes to socializing for an INFJ is when you are recharged, craving interaction, and feeling connected. This is when you come alive and are ready to rock a room. When your sliding scales line up in just this way, it is time to practice your baby steps.

You can make these sliding scales work in your favor once you recognize their existence. You probably already knew the difference between feeling drained and feeling recharged. Seeing it as a sliding scale and noting actions that get you from one side of the scale to the other allows you to schedule these actions and harness this scale. Reading a book, taking a shower, meditating, going for a walk, or snagging a nap are all common ways that an INFJ can shift from drained to recharged.

Depending on how drained you are will depend on the amount of time you need to tip the scale.

Socially satisfied and craving interaction is a scale that may have felt out of your control up until now, but with some practice, you can tip this scale in any direction you wish. You may wonder why you would ever want to crave interaction if you are already feeling socially satisfied. Everyone's situation is different but if you are feeling socially satisfied, you may be more apt to be content with where you are and less apt to want to head out and meet new people. This contentment could come back to bite you later when you are feeling lonely. So sometimes you want to get yourself to a state of craving in order to get out there and connect. To shift from socially satisfied to craving, think of fun activities you enjoy participating in with others. These could be things like dancing, playing a board game, hiking, or any host of things you enjoy. The idea here is to get really excited about the idea of it. Perhaps go back to your visualization technique from earlier about the perfect platonic date. When you feel that excitement, you are more apt to crave it, and once you get to the point that you are craving it, you will want to take action to fulfill it.

It's important to note that it would be unhelpful to try to shift from satisfied to craving when you are feeling drained or lonely. Then you are setting yourself up for emotional disaster. But if you are already feeling recharged and connected, then visualizing to reach that craving may be just what you need to jumpstart yourself.

As we already touched on earlier in this book, you do not need another person to help you feel connected. To go from lonely to connected, you don't need a best friend just yet. Hopping into an online forum and reading through comments of people you relate to allows you to feel connected. Reading through a blog of another that helps you recognize that you are not alone allows you to feel connected. Simply looking to the internet, books, films, or anything that reminds you that there are others who understand you can help you feel connected. Being connected does not have to do with a deep friendship, but rather those moments when you see you are not alone and feel that excitement of being understood. Use the connectedness exercise mentioned earlier in the book when you want assistance going from lonely to connected.

If you wanted to make this connection feel more intimate, go out people watching. Sometimes the act of watching others and noticing their behaviors allows you to feel connected. Author and speaker, Dr. Wayne Dyer, uses the technique of looking at others and noticing their fingernails; seeing that the very thing within them that causes their fingernails to grow also resides within you. Basically, connect at a human level. Look for the areas that you are the same as another. The more you look to your similarities rather than your differences, the more connected you will feel.

Schedule a time when you want to begin practicing approaching strangers and then give yourself an hour or two before that time to balance your scales. Take some time alone to recharge yourself. Feel connected in your humanity. Visualize your favorite social activity. Line up those scales so that you are feeling as close to recharged, connected, and craving interaction as possible. Then head out and get to work practicing your baby steps.

Most people who are able to talk with anyone effortlessly were not born any different than the rest of us. There is nothing inherently ingrained within you that prevents you from approaching strangers, sparking conversation and meeting new people. The only difference between you and those that appear to fluidly converse is simply practice. They have spent a great deal of time practicing approaching others. This practice may have begun at the age of two or at the age of twenty. For myself, I was already in my thirties before I began practicing how to approach strangers and now, when you catch me in the perfect mood with my scales lined up, I can make it look easy.

The same can be true for you with just a little bit of exercise. After a couple of weeks of performing the following baby steps, you will look back and wonder how you ever thought it difficult to spark conversation.

The first baby step begins with one word: "hi." Make it a goal every time you leave the house to say hi to each person you encounter. These could be people walking by you on the street, sitting next to you on a bus, or even a cashier at the supermarket. Every single person you manage to face, simply say hi. Make it feel comfortable and natural to you. Maybe you prefer saying, "Hey" or "what's up?" Any generic greeting paired with a smile will do.

As you go through the day greeting others, notice their responses. You may be surprised to discover that they respond just as naturally. Head nods, smiles, or replies will roll out as if they have done this a million times themselves. You might get one or two people who glare or grimace. Don't let that deter you from continuing. If you say hi to ten people and two grimace, focus on the ease of the eight who enjoyed the encounter.

If you find yourself struggling a great deal with those who offer less than appealing responses, pause for a moment and consider it from their angle. Imagine what type of mood you would need to be in to glare at someone offering you a polite greeting. When you do this, you will realize that their reaction has absolutely nothing to do with you. This takes the sting out and helps you move forward, continuing to say hi to everyone you meet.

After you have done this for a day or two and feel a little less uncomfortable greeting complete strangers (you will be surprised to discover how quickly it becomes comfortable), move on to baby step number two: expand the conversation with at least two people each day. When I say expand, I am not referring to delving in deep, but rather going a little further than a one word greeting. The easiest way to start this step is to practice with cashiers, bank tellers, waiters or anyone who is focused on you already. If you do not receive a grimace after the initial hello, go further in one of two ways:

- Offer them a sincere compliment
- Ask them a question

Rather than waiting until you are in the moment to come up with an opener, I want you to script them ahead of time. Believe it or not, some of the most charismatic and public figures began with scripted conversations. Athletes, actors, celebrity interviewers, and talk show hosts all rely heavily on scripted responses and questions, even to the point of carrying cards with them. When we meet someone new, our brains tend to be in overdrive, so scripting two or three things to say as well as potential follow ups will help you calm the mental chatter and be able to focus your thoughts quickly in any moment. It is important to script things as you would actually say them. The point is to practice being *you* publicly, not pulling stiff one-liners from a book. Compliments can be something like, "oh wow! I love that ring/watch/bag!" or "that was the fastest any cashier has rung me out. Thank you!" Whether you choose to compliment their appearance or actions, be sure that the compliment is genuine, appropriate, and in your own tone.

Compliments are perfect for putting you and the other individual at ease, but they tend to fall off in conversation unless there is something to keep it moving. In this case, tacking on a question can keep the conversation flowing with little effort. If you compliment an item or article of clothing, the easiest follow up is, "may I ask where you got it?" If you compliment their action, ask how they learned it or how they became so good at their craft.

Offering compliments and follow up conversations not only allows you to meet more people than you normally would have, upping your chances of meeting your next best friend, but it also increases your confidence. As your confidence increases, you will feel better with each conversation and others will feel more comfortable around you. As Leil Lowndes, author of *How to Talk to Anyone: 92 Little Tricks for Big Success in Relationships* wrote, "Remember, repeating an action makes a habit. Your habits create your character. And your character is your destiny. May success be your destiny."[8]

Most of us are creatures of habit, walking the same street every day, visiting the same restaurants often, and hitting the same shops on a regular basis. For that reason, you are fairly likely to bump into the same people over and over again. This happens more than we realize since we don't often notice background individuals with any long term remembrance. But once you begin conversing with

BABY STEPS

1 Say "hello" to everyone

2 Expand the conversation

3 Follow up conversation

---

[8] Lowndes, Leil. *How to Talk to Anyone: 92 Little Tricks for Big Success in Relationships.* McGraw-Hill Education; 2 edition; 2003.

these background individuals, you will start to see them pop up again and again. If you find your schedule to be sporadic, leaving you with a different group of people surrounding you every day, try scheduling a couple of hours a week to do the same routine and see if you begin noticing the same people popping up.

Having had a previous conversation, others will start to remember you as well. Baby step number three is to carrying on a conversation with someone you have previous chatted with or complimented. Remember what you discussed and simply bring it up again. If you discussed the speed of a cashier and asked how they got so good at it, next time you see them, follow up with another question based on their previous response. If they said they learned their techniques from an earlier position, ask about that earlier position. Compliment someone's purse? Next time you see them, you could let them know you saw a similar purse at certain store. Again, keep it genuine. Do not lie or stretch for the sake of conversation. If you know you are going to see the same person again, sit and consider what you may follow up with ahead of time. Allow yourself to prepare instead of jumping into the moment.

The majority of people go about their day guarded, hoping someone else will open up first so that they can feel comfortable doing the same. If this is how you feel, than you can recognize that you already have a great deal in common with most of those you encounter. The difference is that you can now recognize it. As an INFJ, you have the gift of seeing people for who they are and reading their subtle cues. This puts you far ahead of the social game when used right. As of right now, that ability to read people may be the very reason you do not want to open up. You can feel their reactions to your every word and movement, causing you to feel scrutinized and lead you to shut down. But what if you changed up the social scenario in a manner that catches the other person so off guard that they don't even have a chance to scrutinize you?

You see, most conversations with strangers are predictable:

- You: "Hi, how's it going?"
- Them: "Great and you?"
- You: "Good."

When you veer from this pattern, people remember you. If you make them feel good, they look forward to seeing you again. Through implementing these three baby steps, scripting your responses ahead of time while remaining genuine to who you are, you start to open up doorways to connections that did not previously exist. Through these open doorways, you allow in more and more people, decreasing your feelings of loneliness and increasing your chances of finding mutual friendships with others just like you.

End Overthinking

"We are dying from overthinking. We are slowly killing ourselves by thinking about everything. Think. Think. Think. You can never trust the human mind anyway. It's a death trap."
Anthony Hopkins

"Most misunderstandings in the world could be avoided if people would simply take the time to ask, 'What else could this mean?'"
Shannon L. Alder

"To think too much is a disease."
Fyodor Dostoyevsky

The stars align, you are feeling great, all of your scales have fallen into place whether through timing or determined effort, and you have a social obligation in the books. Maybe you are nervous, maybe you're excited. You run through the way you hope the night goes, scripting conversations, visualizing the entire evening. The moment arrives and you are excited about the opportunity of a potential future friendship.

No matter how great the night went or how on point you felt you were, you end the evening lying in bed and your brain kicks on. You begin dissecting every aspect of the conversations you held. What they said. What you said. How they said it. What you wish you had said. The way they held their body, every minute facial expression, even the direction they pointed their toes run through your mind as if you keep hit rewind and wearing out an old VHS tape. You consider that one sentence that slipped out that you regret saying or the word you stumbled over or even if you were 100% truthful when you said what kind of music you enjoy. Sleep feels impossible as your brain is in overdrive pondering everything and considering how you will go on the offensive and perform damage control tomorrow.

By the time your brain has slowed, you feel awful. The high of an amazing evening is a distant memory and you now exist in a state of self-loathing, wishing you weren't you. The earlier hope of finding a longtime friend has waned and now you face the reality that you have chased away yet another wonderful person.

The next day you awaken in a state much worse than the first. You feel drained and groggy but still holding the memories of everything you did wrong. Damage control no longer sounds like a good idea as clearly any mode of contacting them would simply annoy them anyway. Instead you go through your day just trying to rest and recharge, checking your phone often to see if they contact you. Days go by and not a peep. You were right. The night was awful.

This vicious cycle, or at least a version of it, is surely familiar. Even if they did contact you to get together again, you continue to follow this same script until they no longer reach out since you are too frightened to reciprocate lest you come across as needy or annoying. Each and every time you go through this cycle, you feel worse and these beliefs about yourself become more deeply ingrained within your subconscious. You not only begin to believe all the negative worries within your mind as they appear proven accurate through the dwindling connection, but you also start to undermine your own ability to read situations. While within the moment you feel like you are on top of the world, connecting and communicating with another like a champ, your reflection on the encounter shows a different viewpoint which leaves you wondering if you were ever reading the situation accurately in the first place. This questioning of your ability worsens over time until you develop a sense of anxiety in communicating with others, overthinking every move and word within the moment, closing yourself off further and further.

If this scenario sounds in any way familiar, then take heart in knowing that you are not the only one experiencing this cycle. And what's better, you can stop it in its tracks and derail to a new mental script which will yield new results.

Susan Nolen-Hoeksema, author of *Women Who Think Too Much: How to Break Free of Overthinking and Reclaim Your Life*, calls this type of overthinking "life-of-their-own thinking."[9]   This, essentially, is when our overthinking causes small problems that do not actually exist. When this happens, it brings about more thoughts which only further prove that our original faulty thought was correct, slowly cycling and taking on a life of its own; one that seems to be based in reality but is in all actuality an overblown fabrication of our mind. Nolen-Hoeksema goes on to point out that this type of thinking can lead to hasty actions: *"We confront others, we decide to quit our job or school, we cancel social outings, acting out of our bad moods and exaggerated concerns."* Basically, overthinking causes us to do things we may regret and isolate us from the very situations we crave.

Remember earlier how we discussed that the people you wish to connect with who are similar to you may have the same fears, hang ups, or worries as you, preventing you from connecting with them? The same applies here. As you find yourself sitting in silence with a rushing mind, odds are that the person you are overthinking about is overthinking about you, too. In a study conducted by Nolen-Hoeksema, she found that

---

[9] Nolen-Hoeksema, Susan. *Women Who Think Too Much: How to Break Free of Overthinking and Reclaim Your Life.* Henry Holt and Co.; 2004.

57% of women and 43% of men are overthinkers. If you fall in the younger categories, those statistics are likely higher. A whopping 73% of people ages 25 to 35 tend to overthink scenarios. As the age increases to 45 to 55 year olds, that percentage drops down to just over half of the population. But take heart in knowing that it only gets better. Individuals 65 years and older are down to a mere 20% of overthinkers. When you consider those numbers, odds are pretty strong that you are not the only one overthinking the evening's interactions. If more than half of the general population is overthinking, just consider how many potential friendships are missed because your thoughts took on a life of their own. So what does this mean for you? It means that most of those people you thought you were annoying probably liked you enough to overthink about you.

On top of being excited to be a part of a statistic that means you are common and not broken, you also can blame your inner workings for your overthinking. A study published in the *Journal of Neuroscience* shows that those such as yourself who fall on the introverted side of the Interpersonal Adjective Scales have thicker gray matter in our prefrontal cortex compared to those who fell on the extroverted side of the scale.[10] This part of one's brain is the hub of abstract thinking, complex planning, impulse control, and organizing varying layers of social interactions. Extroverts, having less gray matter in the area of their prefrontal cortex are more capable of living in the moment. They can take interactions at face value and then move on to the next interaction with very little analysis. Introverts, on the other hand, focus on each implication of their social engagements, pulling from past experiences, societal norms, and a variety of layers of human existence. This not only makes you more cautious in approaching social interactions but also is the cause of your overthinking after it is all said and done. This isn't to say that only introverts struggle with overthinking, but physiologically, we are more prone to such behavior.

---

[10] Holmes, A. J., Lee, P. H., Hollinshead, M. O., et al. "Individual Differences in Amygdala-Medial Prefrontal Anatomy Link Negative Affect, Impaired Social Functioning, and Polygenic Depression Risk." *Journal of Neuroscience*. 12 Dec. 2012: 2 (50) 18087-18100.

DERAIL THE CYCLE

As you can see, you are not alone in the realm of overthinking. This is all well and good, but what can you do to change the way your brain was developed and the hardwiring that has taken place over the course of your life? Through simple awareness and a couple of practiced tricks, it is possible to break free of the overthinking which paralyzes you from attaining the deep friendships you desire. As Nolen-Hoeksema writes:

> "Trying to overcome overthinking is like trying to escape from quicksand. The first step to freedom is to break the grip of your thoughts so that they don't continue to pull you down further, and eventually smother you. The second step is to climb up out of the muck onto higher ground where you can see things more clearly and make good choices about what directions you should go in in the future. The third step is to avoid falling into the trap of overthinking once again."

Breaking the grip of your thoughts is essential to ending the cycle of overthinking. Many of us have cultivated the habit of passively allowing our thoughts to dictate our feelings and actions. It is, in fact, possible to grab ahold of your thoughts, controlling their direction, and ceasing them from taking on a life of their own. Subconscious habits force us into overthinking situations so actively using our conscious mind to decide what we wish to think and therefore believe about our social interactions allows us to stop the cycle before it has a chance to grow larger and seemingly out of our control.

The best way to stop a train of thought before it begins is to start another one. After you leave a social engagement, your brain enjoys rehashing some of the pleasurable moments before it starts noticing the little things that begin the downward spiral. Allow yourself a few minutes of reveling in the emotional high from a great interaction but shift into a new train of thought before you have a chance to overthink too much. You may find it beneficial to set a time limit on your thinking. After ten minutes, move on to other thoughts. In the moment, this shift will feel challenging, so it is best to schedule or preplan something to take your mind off of your thoughts. As an introvert, jumping from one interaction to another is less than ideal so consider something that allows you to relax and recharge while taking enough of your mental energy that you cannot think of how the meeting went. This could be reading a book, exercising, playing a solitary game, listening to music with captivating lyrics, watching a film, or jumping into a project you enjoy.

It is likely that this will feel uncomfortable. Your brain *wants* to think about the interaction and your ego, the piece of your mind that is designed to notice threats and neutralize them, will be shouting at you to pay attention and think deeper into the interaction. Acknowledge your ego for trying to protect you, but remind it that there is no threat here. Our ego functions on an animalistic belief that to be disliked by others is to be shunned from a tribe which used to be the equivalent of death. This is why feeling disliked after an interaction is so painful and worrisome. Look at this part of yourself as an adorable puppy dog who is barking at the potential threat of a mailman. Its intentions are pure and it thinks it is saving you, but you know better and can soothe it back into its place.

As your ego barks for self-protection, ask yourself a couple of questions to help soothe it:

Did you intentionally try to hurt anyone else while you were interacting? The answer here is probably no. In this case, release any worries of how another perceived you. If you find yourself fearing that someone took something you said in the wrong way, then you are worrying about a fact which is outside of your control. As long as you know that your intentions were never to harm, then you can begin to feel at ease about everything that may or may not have come out of your mouth. If the answer is yes, then rather than overthinking, consider how you can make a plan to make amends in the situation and look into why you felt the need to harm.

Did you tell the truth and act in complete integrity to the best of your knowledge in the moment? This one may feel a little gray when you think of a quick response you may have offered which, thinking back, was not as clear or thorough as you would have liked. INFJs love to tell the truth, the whole truth, and nothing but the truth, and it is easy to view omission, even unintentional omission, as not being truthful or authentic. In this case, it is important to note the piece of this question that states "to the best of your knowledge in the moment." Odds are that your intention was never to lie or omit any information. You communicated in the purest manner you were capable of at the time.

With these two questions answered and soothed, you allow your ego to relax as you recognize that you acted in accordance with your true self within the moment and there was nothing you could have done better. The way in which you were perceived or the opinion of whoever you engaged with is not within your control and therefore is not worth stressing over for hours on end. Just as acknowledging a puppy's bark and soothing it back into place, being grateful for its attempt to protect you, you can acknowledge your ego's fears, recognize that it is trying to keep you safe, and calm it by reminding yourself that there is no threat at the present time.

With a soothed ego, you are now capable of focusing on another task to take your mind off of the overthinking. Make sure you are not doing exhausting busy work that will drain you. The idea is not to avoid thinking or feeling in general, but to shift you to thoughts and feelings that are beneficial to you. By doing tasks that you enjoy and take thought away from overthinking, you allow yourself to recharge and come into a more positive frame of mind before your thoughts run away from you.

At some point, you will find yourself thinking about the encounter. In these moments, make an active effort to only think of the facts. With the two earlier questions answered, do not allow your mind to enter what is called mind reading cognitive distortion. This is a type of thinking which distorts reality in a negative and unhealthy manner by assuming you know what another is thinking. Thoughts like, *they must find me so annoying* or *she probably thinks I'm crazy* are examples of mind reading cognitive distortion. If you find yourself veering from the facts and noticing yourself mind reading, take a moment to write down exactly what you think the other person thought of you. Sometimes simply writing it down can show you how ludicrous of a thought it is. If you still cannot help but believe it to be true, consider the factual evidence for or against this statement. Think back on the encounter and write down what made you believe this thought. Did the other person make a comment or facial expression that caused you to come to this conclusion? Was it one thing or several things? Now look at the whole of the night. Did their behavior act consistently in line with this thought or were there just one or two instances that seem to point to it?

Make sure your evidence is completely factual. Following up a mind reading belief with another mind reading belief will only perpetuate the negative cycle of overthinking, leading it to take on a life of its own. Instead, look at only what you know. Things like, *they spent most of the night looking at their phone* is a fact. *They spent most of their night avoiding me* is mind reading. The differences may seem subtle, but one is based on reality

EVIDENCE EXAMPLE

Mind reading belief: They thought I was annoying.

Proof of assumption: They didn't ask me any questions when I talked about work.

Proof against assumption: They didn't walk away or make an excuse to leave. They did initiate a conversation about [...]. They laughed when I made a joke.

while the other assumes intent. *They held eye contact with me often* is a fact. *They were staring at me because they think I am weird* is distorted mind reading.

After you have written down the facts surrounding your belief, ask yourself if it would hold up in court. Is it possible that they weren't thinking what you think they were thinking? Is their reasonable doubt that they may, in fact, not find you annoying? By focusing only on the facts as you think back on your interactions and identifying when you may be using cognitive distortion will help you control your thoughts and allow you to shift your default thinking methods, breaking the cycle and allowing you to see the situation in a new light.

As you begin to break out of overthinking, you can more clearly assess reality as it is and plan your next steps accordingly. Think back to that worry of not contacting someone after meeting with them because you are scared they didn't actually like you or that you would be annoying to them. You wait and wait, hoping that they contact you first. In the instances when they do contact you first, you make another meeting, overthink that meeting, and then worry again about contacting them because surely they must be sick of you by now. Overtime this distorted thinking will push others away as they feel like the friendship is one-sided. At some point, you need to break through and be the contactor instead of waiting to be the contactee.

Much the same as learning to initiate conversations with strangers, learning how to reach out to others takes practice and baby steps. You will feel a little uncomfortable as you start out but overtime and through assessing the facts of reality, your confidence will grow and you will shift into a place where you feel comfortable reaching out to someone when something is on your mind.

Think of how it feels to know that someone else is thinking of you. Feel that warm, fuzzy emotion that brews inside of you when someone sends you a note that shows, not only were they thinking about you, but something they saw, heard, or read made you come to mind. It feels good to be noticed. Now consider the times that you wanted to reach out to someone else to let them know you were thinking of them. Did you second guess yourself or hold back? What were your fears? Were you worried they would find it creepy or annoying that you would be thinking of them? Maybe you felt vulnerable opening yourself up to someone who may not have been thinking about you. Now what if you break through and send it anyway? What is the worst that could happen?

This is how friendships are formed, through small communications, remembrances, and notes letting one another see that they have been heard and respected. With each communication, these feelings grow and comfort increases. If we withhold from offering these smaller communications out of fear due to our mind reading distortions, the odds of fostering long term healthy relationships are significantly low. When I asked what is the worst that could happen, you probably shifted to worry of what they would think of you or that they would respond in a way that confirmed your fear that they do not like you. If this happens, then feel good knowing that you can now shift your energy towards another person. As Thomas Watson, Sr., the founder of IBM, once said, "The fastest way to succeed is to double your failure rate." Through taking action forward in friendship, you can learn much faster whether it is worth pursuing or abandoning.

After an encounter with someone, if you see something or think of something that brings them to mind, go ahead and reach out. Social media and our online connections have made this easier than ever. Instead of having to walk to their home and knock on their door, or even the dreaded discomfort of picking up a phone, now you can communicate with the click of a button. A quick text, an article or image share, or a goofy photo complete with filter sent their way can bridge the gap between uncomfortable worrying and relationship building.

From here, you can move onto inviting them somewhere. This does not have to be a grand gesture and there are ways to soften the invite for the comfort of both parties involved. Rather than thinking of a grandiose invitation hinging on their response, try something like, "I was thinking of heading to the park for a walk today and wondered if you were free to join me?" Or "I am going to be out shopping and was wondering if you wanted to grab lunch?" This softens the invite because the plans do not hinge on whether or not the other person is available to accept. If they decline, you still have something to do. If they accept, that something just got better. This also helps if they are overthinkers. If they genuinely cannot attend, then they are relieved of the guilt of thinking they ruined your day or your plans.

There are no rules or games here. You can just do what you feel comfortable with doing. Do not put the burden of reading another's mind in your court. If someone is not interested in pursuing a friendship with you, then they will not reciprocate or they will tell you they are unable to get together. In the case that a friendship does not pan out, you can go back to the earlier exercise of connectedness to remind yourself that you are in no rush to find that perfect friendship and you are confident that it will come in due time. There are plenty of other people out there and, as you can tell, quite a few of them think just like you.

You Are the Only You

"Always remember that you are absolutely unique. Just
like everyone else."
Margaret Mead

"Always be yourself, express yourself, have faith in
yourself, do not go out and look for a successful
personality and duplicate it."
Bruce Lee

"To help yourself, you must be yourself. Be the best that
you can be. When you make a mistake, learn from it,
pick yourself up and move on."
Dave Pelzer

You are a unique individual. No one in the world is exactly like you. You have your own thoughts, your own feelings, your own distinctive viewpoint, and your own intricate past that has woven together to create you. This will never change. There will never be another you. There are many out there who are looking for someone just like you. They will be different and they will see life in their own unique way, regardless of whether you share the same Myers-Briggs letters. They will be uniquely them and different from everyone else that you meet. Every single one of us is different. This does not prevent us from establishing meaningful, lifelong connections with those around us.

Each and every one of us can connect with others on a variety of levels and a variety of topics. The more you expand the number of people you encounter and interact with, the more opportunities you have to create meaningful connections in a variety of ways. There are at least 75 million INFJs in the world. There are even more who are familiar with and love discussing Myers-Briggs. There a billions who enjoy the same hobbies, see the same movies, read the same books, and drink the same tea. And every single person's fingernails grow in the same fashion.

The opportunities to connect with others are endless once you change your perspective of how you fit into the world and practice reaching out to each person you meet. You are the only you and that is what makes you a hot commodity in the field of companionship. But just as a popular brand cannot become a commodity hidden away in a basement, you cannot become a friend if you hide inside of yourself.

Take the time to find personal fulfillment in what you bring to the table. Establish how you want to feel in the ideal friendship, visualizing what you want, and fine-tuning everything you are seeking. You deserve to have the friendship of your dreams and there millions out there who will fit your criteria. Use a soft opener and, as you allow yourself to become more and more visible, begin connecting with complete strangers. Through taking these steps and paying close attention to how you feel and where you fall on the sliding scales, you will gradually begin to harness the strengths that have been lying dormant within you and begin opening yourself to a whole new world of relationships.

From here, look around at those around you, see the billions of people in the world connecting, communicating, and even those hiding, and reach out, make yourself accessible, and allow yourself the opportunity to finally make some real connections.

ALSO LOOK FOR

The Empathic INFJ:
Awareness and Understanding for the
Intuitive Clairsentient

This book, when paired with *The Empathic INFJ Workbook: Tools and Strategies for the Intuitive Clairsentient*, will offer you a functional and focused guide to understanding your level of empathic abilities and help you learn and establish new tools and techniques to thrive in your day to day living.

Complete with descriptions, resources and tools, grab you copy today!

The INFJ Heart:
Understand the Mind, Unlock the Heart

A look into the inner workings of an INFJ, this book brings your relationship to the front and center, helping you to understand the INFJ in your life. Also great for an INFJ looking to delve deeper into how their personality directly relates to their ability to communicate and connect with those around them.

By achieving a deeper understanding of this unique personality, you may be one of the lucky few to unlock the secrets of the INFJ heart.

For more information about these works as well as future publications, please visit jennifersoldner.com.